To:

....

From:

....

Other books in this series

Mother's Love

Love You, Dad

True Love

Friends Forever

42 Ways to Celebrate Love, Loyalty, and Togetherness

ANNE ROGERS SMYTH

NATIONAL
GEOGRAPHIC

WASHINGTON, D.C.

PUBLISHED BY THE NATIONAL GEOGRAPHIC SOCIETY

1145 17th Street N.W., Washington, D.C. 20036

ISBN: 978-1-4262-1368-7

The National Geographic Society is one of the world's largest nonprofit scientific and educational organizations. Its mission is to inspire people to care about the planet. Founded in 1888, the Society is member supported and offers a community for members to get closer to explorers, connect with other members, and help make a difference. The Society reaches more than 450 million people worldwide each month through *National Geographic* and other magazines; National Geographic Channel; television documentaries; music; radio; films; books; DVDs; maps; exhibitions; live events; school publishing programs; interactive media; and merchandise. National Geographic has funded more than 10,000 scientific research, conservation, and exploration projects and supports an education program promoting geographic literacy. For more information, visit www.nationalgeographic.com.

National Geographic Society
1145 17th Street N.W.
Washington, D.C. 20036-4688 U.S.A.

For information about special discounts for bulk purchases, please contact National Geographic Books Special Sales: ngspecsales@ngs.org

For rights or permissions inquiries, please contact National Geographic Books Subsidiary Rights: ngbookrights@ngs.org

Interior design: Melissa Farris

Printed in Hong Kong

14/THK/1

*To my good friends near
and far, you make
everything better*

A good friend **has your back**—again and again and again.

Though often called the koala "bear," this cuddly animal is actually a marsupial, or pouched mammal, that uses its pouch to carry young for up to six months after giving birth.

Your true colors shine brightest in the company of a good friend.

❧

The red-eyed tree frog uses its bright blue-and-yellow flanks, huge orange toes, and lustrous neon green body to overstimulate keen-eyed predators.

Good friends see
eye to eye, no matter
how different they are.

Despite their disparate statures, all dogs are believed to have evolved from gray wolves.
Diversification occurred as man bred them to perform different tasks.

Brushing off embarrassment **is** easier with a good friend around.

No two tigers have the same stripes, but their distinctive coats help them blend in with the filtered jungle sunlight and hunt in stealth.

Loyalty **runs deep**
with good friends.

*Horses' highly developed nervous systems and fine senses
of smell and hearing enable them to find their way home
even after a prolonged absence.*

A good friend never
lets you settle for the path
of **least resistance.**

With their thick skin, stout bodies, and tusklike teeth, pigs are known for
their ability to find food resources and to survive in almost any environment.

Elephants' ears radiate heat to help regulate body temperature, but in times of extreme heat, they use their trunks to suck up water and release a refreshing spray.

A good friend is there
to help you **keep your cool.**

There's no such thing
as a bad hair day
in the **eyes of a good friend.**

Alpacas live in social herds that act as families, protecting and caring for each other.
They often hum to one other as a form of communication.

For **much needed relaxation,** chill out with good friends.

*Polar bears sleep for seven to eight hours at a time,
and they are known to nap just about anywhere and anytime
to conserve energy, particularly after feeding.*

When you're feeling blue,
a good friend is there to remind you
that you're **never alone.**

Chameleons change color not to match their surroundings, but rather to communicate with each other and to indicate specific reactions and emotions.

A good friend is the best
partner in crime.

Named for their unusually fluffy, silklike plumage, Silkies are known for their easy,
friendly personalities and are considered to be ideal pets.

If you're stuck,
a good friend will
come running.

In addition to seeking out fresh pasture,
inquisitive cattle investigate anything new or
different in their environment.

A good friend is
an **unexpected** soul mate.

∞

Not unlike its canine companion, the white-tailed deer displays and wags its tail when on alert.
Known for its superior speed and agility, it leaps as high as 10 feet (3 m) in a single bound.

A good friend **stays by your side**
as long as you need.

*A typical panda eats for half the day—a full 12 out of every 24 hours—and consumes
up to 28 pounds (12.5 kg) of bamboo to satisfy its daily dietary needs.*

If the whole world feels upside-down,
a good friend can help you
change your perspective.

One of the few bat species that doesn't use echolocation, the fruit bat relies on large eyes
to orient itself visually in twilight and inside caves and forests.

~ 37 ~

A good friend doesn't need
words to communicate—
one look can **say it all.**

For protection, gregarious weaver birds often build their elaborately woven
(hence the name) nests together, sometimes several to a branch.

When you need to talk,
a good friend
is **all ears.**

Rabbits, whose long ears give them a super-heightened sense of hearing,
are relatively silent—which makes them even better listeners.

A good friend keeps you heading
in the **right direction.**

*Graceful and slender schooling bannerfish gather along outer reef slopes
and in current channels in warm waters.*

A good friend is always
in on the joke.

∞

The snowy owl's magnificent white plumage helps it hide in its Arctic habitat,
though only the males are completely white. Females are slightly darker with dusky spotting.

Both sides of a situation
are clear to a good friend.

Notorious hoarders, chipmunks are constantly searching for insects, nuts, berries, seeds, and grain,
which they stuff into their generous cheek pouches and carry to their burrow to store.

A good friend will always
stick her neck out for you.

The world's tallest mammals, giraffes roam the open grasslands in
small groups of about a half dozen. They spend most of their time eating.

Whatever the situation, a good friend
reminds you to **keep your chin up.**

With a spinal column held together by muscles rather than by ligaments, cats have
incredible flexibility and are so coordinated that they almost invariably land on their feet.

A good friend will
go out on a limb for you.

Highly dexterous front feet that resemble slender human hands
contribute to raccoons' nimbleness and ability to nab food.

Laughter is the language
of good friends.

∞

Lions are the only cats that live in groups, called prides. Female lions are the pride's primary hunters and often work together to catch their prey.

A good friend always knows
which way the party is.

∞

To cope with frigid temperatures, penguins huddle together and take turns
moving to the group's protected and relatively toasty interior.

A good friend brings out your **softer side.**

∞

Sheep are flock animals and have a tendency to stick close together.
They often follow a single leader and move as a unit.

When you're **bugging out,**
a good friend knows
just what to do.

The name mantis, which means "diviner," was given to this insect by
the ancient Greeks because they believed that it had supernatural powers.

A little **silliness**
goes a long way
with good friends.

Living together in groups known as pods,
playful beluga whales blow
bubble rings for amusement.

Your secrets are **always safe**
with a good friend.

Drill monkeys, which are highly endangered, live in small groups with one dominant male and up to 20 females. Sometimes the groups come together to form troops of more than 100.

A good friend is the
yin to your yang.

∞

A zebra's stripes are as unique as fingerprints—no two are exactly alike, and the distinction may help zebras recognize one another.

A moment's notice is all
a good friend needs
to **hop to your side.**

Traveling in groups called mobs, kangaroos use their powerful hind legs, which can move only in tandem, to hop at speeds of more than 35 miles (56 km) an hour.

A good friend
isn't nosy but
asks **all the right**
questions.

❦

The toucan's bright, oversize bill
is mostly for show: It's a honeycomb
of bone that actually contains a lot of air.

Hugs are a good friend's
greatest gift.

In addition to low chatter, clicking, and the occasional high-pitched yell, monkeys use
nonverbal forms of communication—like snuggling and touching faces—to show emotion.

Going with the flow
is easy with good friends.

∞

*Often found floating at the water's surface in serene repose,
sea otters will wrap themselves in kelp for anchorage.*

A good friend is the
luckiest find of all.

Ladybugs' distinctive spots and attractive colors are meant to make them unappealing to predators,
but these features actually make many people fond of them.

Time flies when you're
chatting with a good friend.

*Puffins live in large colonies on coasts and islands and are known for forming
long-term bonds, and couples often reunite at the same nesting spot each year.*

A good friend laughs with you—
and **at you.**

Rarely staying still, gerbils are expert diggers that create elaborate tunnel systems when left in the wild.
A sharp sense of smell helps them identify fellow members of their clan.

Good friends are
always in tune
with one another.

A very thirsty camel can drink 30 gallons (113.5 L)
of water in only 13 minutes. It slurps up the water
and stores it for later sustenance.

A good friend knows
when to **give you a little space.**

*Chihuahuas have a tendency to tremble or shiver when excited or stressed.
Fiercely loyal, they enjoy the companionship of other Chihuahuas.*

A good friend knows it's **about the ride,** not the destination.

True to its name the Hercules beetle is a friend you want on your side:
It can lift up to 850 times its own body weight.

True comfort is found
on the shoulder of a good friend.

Curious and exceptionally agile, goats will go to great heights
to escape enclosure—including climbing trees.

A good friend
looks out for you,
no matter what.

*Meerkats work together in large numbers,
with a few serving as lookouts that survey the sky for
birds of prey and warn the others with a shrill call.*

Illustrations Credits

Front Cover, Stuart Westmorland/Getty Images; Back Cover, Image Source/Corbis; 5, photodeti/iStockphoto; 8-9, Mitsuaki Iwago/Minden Pictures/National Geographic Creative; 10, Peter Reijners/Shutterstock; 13, Tetra Images/Corbis; 14-15, konmesa/Shutterstock; 16-17, gadagj/iStockphoto; 19, mikedabell/iStockphoto; 20-21, Johan Swanepoel/Shutterstock; 22, Alexandra Giese/Shutterstock; 24-25, JohnPitcher/iStockphoto; 27, Sebastian Duda/Shutterstock; 28, Jorge Salcedo/Shutterstock; 30-31, prestongeorge/iStockphoto; 33, Image Source/Corbis; 34-35, WILDLIFE GmbH/Alamy; 36, Universal Images Group Limited/Alamy; 39, Evan McBride/National Geographic Your Shot; 40-41, 4FR/iStockphoto; 42-43, Tim Laman/National Geographic Creative; 45, dean bertoncelj/Shutterstock; 46, Betsy Seeton/National Geographic Your Shot; 49, Anna Omelchenko/Shutterstock; 50-51, Konrad Wothe/Minden Pictures/National Geographic Creative; 52-53, Klein-Hubert/Kimball Stock; 55, Randy Rimland/Shutterstock; 56-57, kwest/Shutterstock; 58, tratong/Shutterstock; 61, gene1988/iStockphoto; 62-63, Hiroya Minakuchi/Minden Pictures/National Geographic Creative; 64, Joel Sartore/National Geographic Stock; 66-67, Bart Martens/Shutterstock; 68, Theo Allofs/Minden Pictures/Corbis; 70-71, holbox/Shutterstock; 73, Hung Chung Chih/Shutterstock; 74-75, Frans Lanting/National Geographic Creative; 76, zorani/iStockphoto; 79, RollingEarth/iStockphoto; 80, Coffeemill/Shutterstock; 82-83, Blend_Images/iStockphoto; 85, Annette Shaff/Shutterstock; 86-87, Nicolas Reusens; 88, aydinmutlu/iStockphoto; 90-91, Ocean/Corbis; 93, adogslifephoto/iStockphoto.